Maps to Bike Gettysburg

No. 2

Battle Day 1 Loop

10.5 miles

Sue Thibodeau

A Companion Mini-Book for
Bicycling Gettysburg National Military Park

Maps to Bike Gettysburg No. 2:
Battle Day 1 Loop (10.5 miles)

Copyright © 2021 Sue Thibodeau

All Rights Reserved. No part of this publication may be reproduced, stored in an archival or retrieval system, distributed, or transmitted, in any form or by any means, including electronic or mechanical means, except in the case of brief quotations embodied in critical reviews and certain other non-commercial uses permitted by copyright law, without the prior written permission of the author.

Map Rendering Copyright © 2019 Sue Thibodeau
Map Data Copyright © OpenStreetMap contributors
www.openstreetmap.org/copyright
Liberation Sans Font Family, SIL Open Font License 1.1

Published by Civil War Cycling
154 Cobblestone Court Drive #110, Victor, NY 14564
Digital (PDF) maps sold separately at civilwarcycling.com

No Warranty. This book is distributed in the hope that it will be useful, but without any warranty, not even an implied warranty of merchantability or fitness for a particular purpose. Consult your doctor before bicycling. The directions provided in this book are for planning purposes only. Actual conditions (road, traffic, weather, or other events) may require you to adjust your route or actions, especially as needed to obey all laws, signs, alerts, and notices. If there are mistakes in this book, or if the park road network or policies have changed since this writing, it remains your responsibility always to act in ways that are safe, healthy, and legal. The author and publisher disclaim any and all liability. Please visit www.nps.gov/gett for official and up-to-date information about park roads, amenities, and policies.

ISBN 978-1-7326038-6-8 (pbk)

20210325-L3-1.2
First Printing

Maps to Bike Gettysburg No. 2: Battle Day 1 Loop (10.5 miles) is a mini-book that complements Civil War Cycling's comprehensive, 286-page guidebook for a 23.8-mile tour:

*Bicycling Gettysburg National Military Park:
The Cyclist's Civil War Travel Guide*
ISBN 978-1-7326038-0-6 (March 2019)

"Whether you're a cycling enthusiast, history buff, or both, Sue Thibodeau's *Bicycling Gettysburg National Military Park: The Cyclist's Civil War Travel Guide* is a must-have for your next visit to Gettysburg. In fact, this 286-page book is so chock-full of useful maps, photographs, and reference information about the battlefield's monuments, farm buildings, and areas of interest that it should be in the daypack of anybody touring the park and/or town of Gettysburg."

~ *Civil War Times*

"*Bicycling Gettysburg* is comprehensible to readers and riders of all ages and expertise... concise and readable for both aficionados and novices."

~ *Civil War Monitor*

"The best ways to truly see a battlefield are by walking and biking. And biking a battlefield such as Gettysburg provides a rush like no other. Sue has produced a valuable book about how to ride that most hallowed Civil War ground. A definite keeper."

~ John Banks, journalist, blogger, author

About the Author

Sue Thibodeau is a bicycling enthusiast, computer scientist, and former teacher. "Like a kid on a bike," she explores U.S. national military parks as a way to learn Civil War history. A graduate of Duke University, the University of Notre Dame, and the Rochester Institute of Technology, Sue publishes educational touring materials through Civil War Cycling.

She is the author of *Bicycling Gettysburg National Military Park* (2019); *Bicycling Antietam National Battlefield* (2020); and two forthcoming guidebooks, *Bicycling Chickamauga Battlefield* (2021) and *Bicycling Shiloh National Military Park* (2022).

About this Book

Maps to Bike Gettysburg No. 2: Battle Day 1 Loop provides color maps and turn-by-turn directions for a safe and educational, 10.5-mile park ride to visit the most famous landmarks of the July 1, 1863 battlefield—including East Cemetery Hill and nearby Culp's Hill. Designed for a lightweight ride, this book complements Civil War Cycling's more detailed and comprehensive guidebook, *Bicycling Gettysburg National Military Park.*

Maps to Bike Gettysburg No. 2 contains 15 detailed color maps with corresponding bicycle cue tables; 45 color photos; monument GPS points; and micro-histories for learning about the Battle of Gettysburg. It is a proper subset of Route 1, but does not 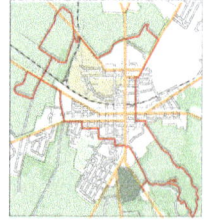 duplicate the guidebook's chapters on tour planning ideas; orienteering techniques; battle statistics; historical summaries; or monument descriptions for a 23.8-mile ride. This mini-book is an expanded print version of the Route 2 digital PDF map that is available at www.civilwarcycling.com/shop/.

This route is ideal for bicyclists who want to ride the entire battlefield in two half-day rides (Route 2 then 3). It covers East Cemetery Hill, McPherson's Ridge, Oak Hill, and Barlow's Knoll. It ends with a bonus tour of Confederate and Union positions around Culp's Hill. Plan for a 3–4-hour ride with frequent stops to get oriented using this book's landscape tips, and to visit some of the park's 1,300+ monuments. This route provides tips for riding on busy public roads; offers route-specific health and safety tips; identifies one-way roads; and notes the location of bicycle racks, water sources, restrooms, and picnic areas.

CONTENTS

Preface	9
1. **Getting Your Mind In Gear**	13
The Battle of Gettysburg (1863)	13
Gettysburg National Military Park	20
Battle Day 1 Loop (No. 2)	22
2. **Let's Go! Bike Route 2**	27
Route 2 Synopsis	27
Similarities Between Routes 1–3	27
Segment A (East Cemetery Hill)	28
Segment B (The Ridge to Oak Hill)	34
Segment C (Return to Tower)	42
Segment D (Barlow's Knoll)	46
Bonus Map—Downtown Gettysburg	51
Segment E (Culp's Hill Area)	52
3. **What Next?**	59

Preface

For more than thirty years, and over many dozens of visits, I toured Gettysburg National Military Park by bus, car, and foot. In 2012, I toured the battlefield on a bicycle for the first time. The experience of learning American history while exploring park land on a bicycle is hard to describe, but if I had to pick one word, it would be "exhilarating." And yet it took four years to work out the kinks in my self-directed, solo tours. I was frustrated by one-way roads, incomplete or inaccurate maps, and not knowing how best to avoid town traffic. But I looked forward to every trip, and enjoyed them all.

Map P.1. Gettysburg, Pennsylvania

Gettysburg National Military Park

Eventually, I learned what equipment to pack, what clothes to wear, and where to find convenient access to water, portable toilets, and shade for picnics. It was also challenging to know how best to sequence my visitation of monuments and within what general timeframe. I created my own maps (and guidebook) because I could not find any maps that met the needs of a bicycling historian. I hope that these maps help you to avoid the mistakes that I had made and that you can enjoy every minute of your battlefield tour.

In September 2018, I designed twelve digital PDF document maps that collectively define fourteen bicycle loops through the Gettysburg battlefield. The maps are available for secure online purchase and download from the Civil War Cycling website. Note: These digital files are not part of a GPS navigation system, and you will need Adobe's free PDF reader to view or print the maps and directions for your Gettysburg cycling tour.

Route #	Route Name	Miles
1	Full Day Loop	23.8
1b	Full Day Short Loop	11.5
2	**Battle Day 1 Loop**	**10.5**
3	Battle Days 2 & 3 Loop	17.0
3b	Battle Days 2 & 3 Short Loop	10.7
4	The Ridges Loop	9.0
5	The Ridges Extended Loop	12.2
6,7	Culp's Hill Lower & Upper Loops	2.4 (ea)
8	Culp's Hill Double Loop	5.5
9–11	Devil's Den, The Wheatfield, and Little Round Top Loops	1.5–3.8
12	East Cavalry Field	5.2

Table of Gettysburg Bicycle Routes

For descriptions and details, visit Civil War Cycling at www.civilwarcycling.com/battlefields/gettysburg/routes/.

Given the popularity of the digital maps—and their appeal to bicyclists who want specifically themed historical rides over varying distances—I launched a paperback mini-book series in 2021 called *Maps to Bike Gettysburg*. Each mini-book is part of an independently usable set of educational publications. They are an expanded subset of Civil War Cycling's comprehensive guidebook for a 23.8-mile tour, *Bicycling Gettysburg National Military Park* (2019).

Maps to Bike Gettysburg No. 2 is one book in a short series of highly focused and portable travel guides. It provides maps, GPS points, monument photos, and micro-histories for Route 2, "Battle Day 1 Loop," a 10.5-mile ride through the Gettysburg battlefield park. As its name suggests, it covers the northern half of the battlefield, especially East Cemetery Hill, Herbst Woods, McPherson's Ridge, Oak Hill, and Barlow's Knoll. In addition, you will ride south on East Confederate Avenue to Spangler's Spring, and then up Culp's Hill via Slocum Avenue.

My hope is that the *Maps to Bike Gettysburg* mini-book series will appeal to bicyclists who want short but detailed printed maps and bicycling directions for a variety of routes. Most bicyclists who enjoy learning history on two wheels will want to return to Gettysburg for many more rides. "Maps to Bike Gettysburg" gives you that option.

Gettysburg National Military Park

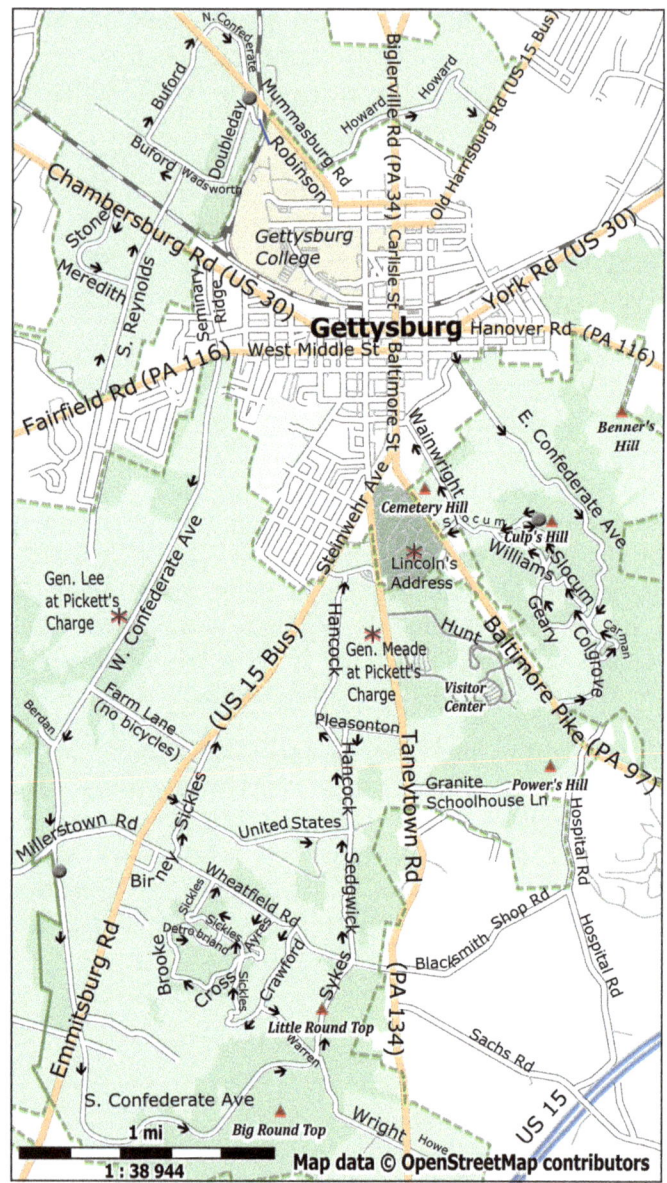

Map P.2. Gettysburg Park Roads

1. Getting Your Mind In Gear

Many people feel a strong desire to visit and then return again to Gettysburg. We struggle to explain our connection to the land and the people who lived and died here. While exploring the battlefield park on two wheels, bicyclists know well the extraordinary feeling that Joshua Chamberlain described in 1889:

In great deeds something abides. On great fields something stays. Forms change and pass; bodies disappear, but spirits linger, to consecrate ground for the vision-place of souls. And reverent men and women from afar, and generations that know us not and that we know not of, heart-drawn to see where and by whom great things were suffered and done for them, shall come to this deathless field to ponder and dream... ~Col. Joshua Lawrence Chamberlain, "Dedication of the 20th Maine Monuments," October 3, 1889, Gettysburg.

This book will take you on a bicycle tour that allows the monuments and the Gettysburg landscape to teach you Civil War history. As a mini-book, it is deliberately brief and yet packed with color maps and turn-by-turn directions for a 10.5-mile bike ride. For a full educational experience, the reader is encouraged to consult Civil War Cycling's comprehensive guidebook, *Bicycling Gettysburg National Military Park*.

The Battle of Gettysburg (1863)

In 1863, Gen. Robert E. Lee and his Confederate Army of Northern Virginia invaded Pennsylvania through Maryland and bore down on Gettysburg from the north. To meet the threat, the newly promoted Maj.

Gettysburg National Military Park

Gen. George G. Meade rallied the Union Army of the Potomac and advanced toward Gettysburg from the south. About 170,000 soldiers converged on this farming town, home to roughly 2,400 citizens, ten miles north of the Maryland border. After three days of fighting on July 1–3, Lee's army was defeated but allowed to retreat back to Virginia. It was the deadliest battle in U.S. military history:

	Union	Confederate	Total
Dead:	3,155	3,903	7,058
Wounded:	14,529	18,735	33,264
Missing/Captured:	5,365	5,425	10,790
Total:	23,049	28,063	51,112

Table 1.1. Gettysburg Casualties

Source: American Battlefield Trust, battlefields.org/learn/civil-war/battles/gettysburg.

A Visual Summary of the Battle—Five Maps

The next five pages summarize the Battle of Gettysburg as a sequence of five military maps. These maps are *deliberately impressionistic* and designed for the overall purpose of learning on-the-go. (Please consult a military atlas if you require more detail).

Army-level battle lines have a blurred look to suggest approximate positions that a bicyclist can commit to memory without having to juggle the names of corps, divisions, or regiments. Union lines are blue and Confederate lines are red. Military positions overlay a modern road network so that bicyclists can easily orient themselves on the battlefield and also understand the high-level battle narrative in the context of one's current location.

July 1, 1863—Wednesday

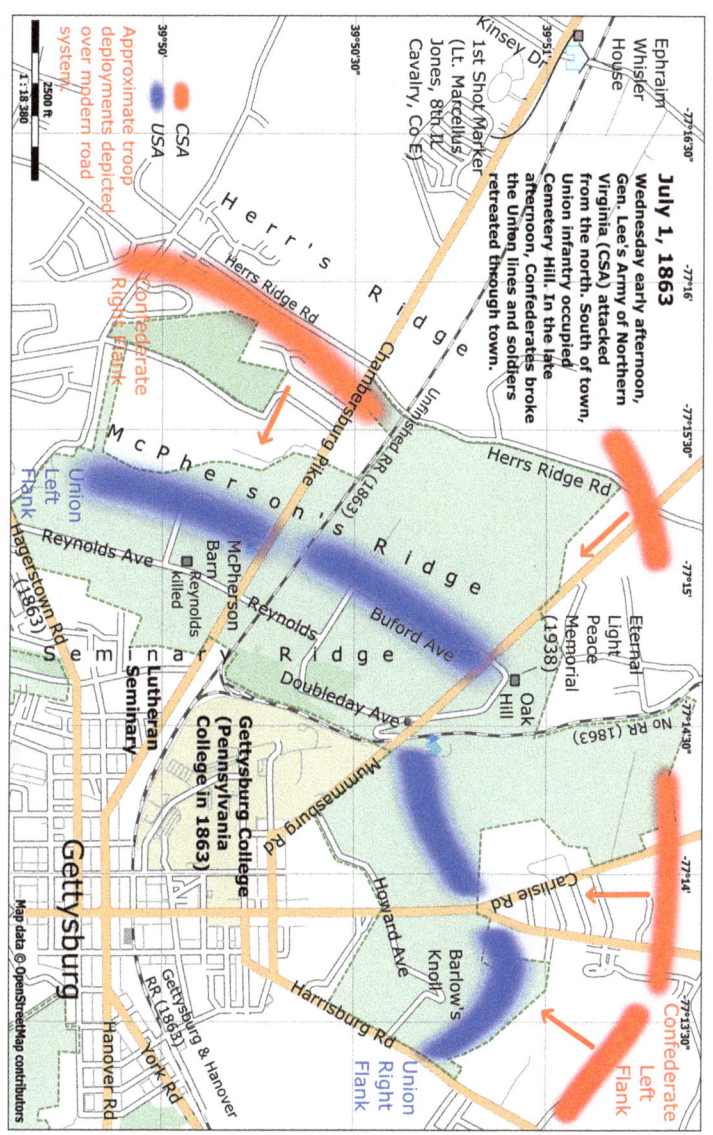

Map 1.1. July 1—Wednesday

Gettysburg National Military Park

July 2, 1863—Thursday

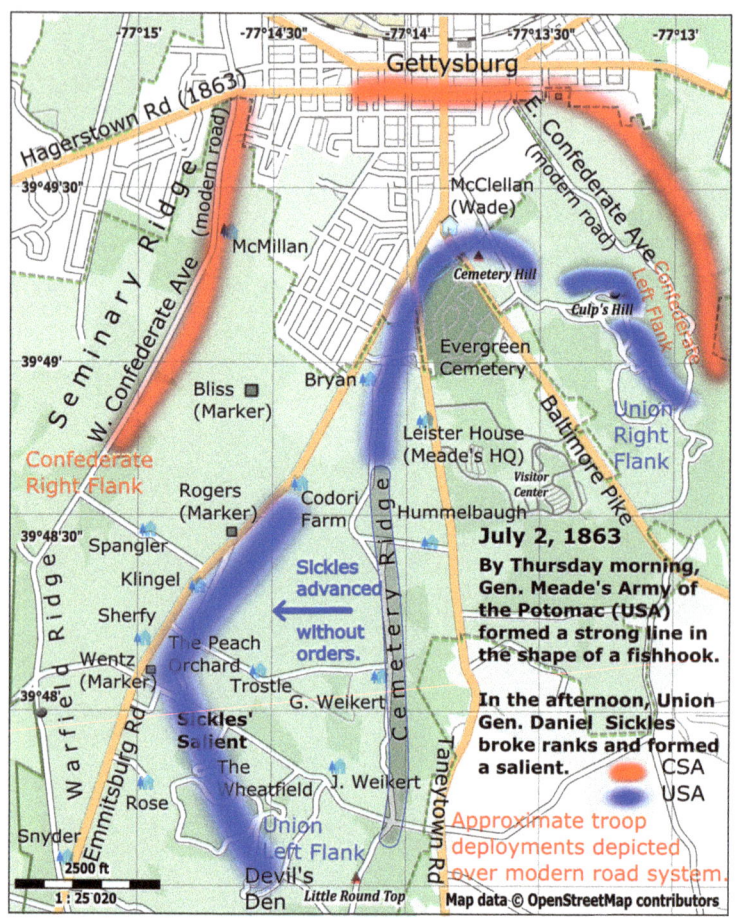

Map 1.2. July 2—Thursday Morning

You will ride down Confederate positions along modern-day East Confederate Avenue; and then up a steep incline that traces Union positions on Culp's Hill. From the observation tower at the summit, look for some of the landmarks identified in the above map.

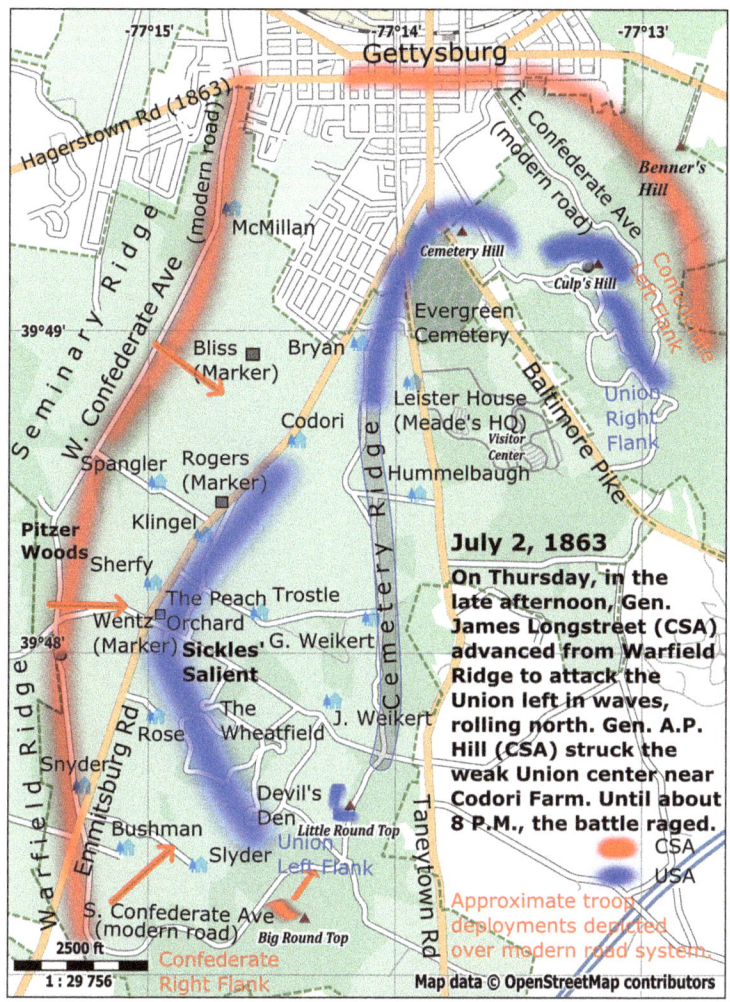

Map 1.3. July 2—Thursday Thursday Late Afternoon

Route 2 does not cover the Confederate attack from Seminary Ridge to Cemetery Ridge on July 2 and 3, 1863. Therefore, if this is your first trip to Gettysburg, you are encouraged to watch the 30-minute movie at the Visitor Center before riding the battlefield.

Gettysburg National Military Park

July 2 & 3, 1863—Battle for Culp's Hill

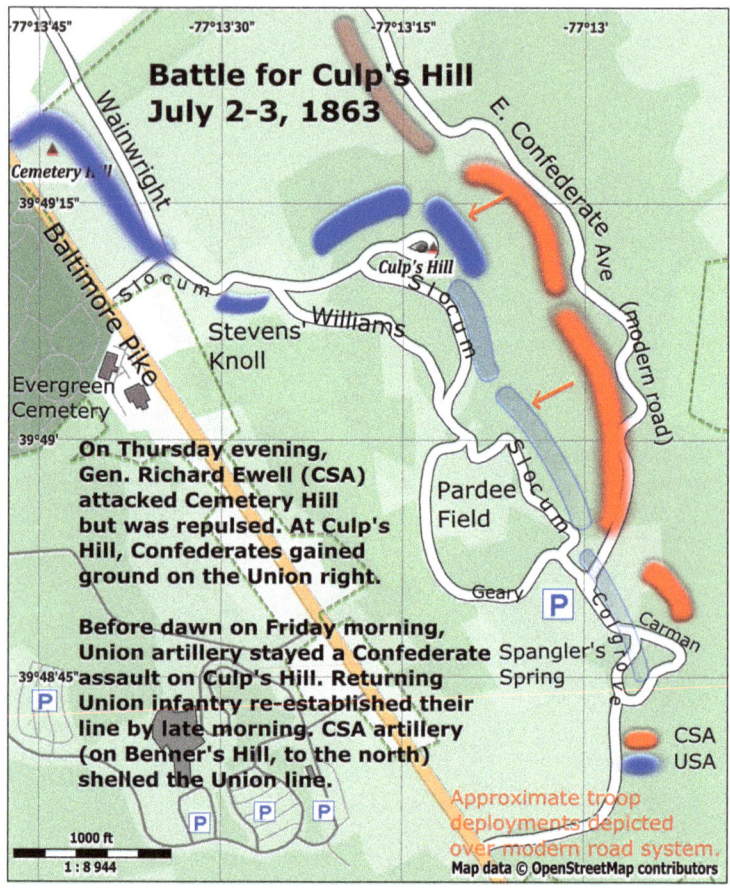

Map 1.4. July 2 and 3—Battle for Culp's Hill

Touring busses are not permitted in the Culp's Hill area, and the ride is not part of the official auto tour. For bicyclists, this less well known historic site offers a beautiful but steep up and down ride. Route 2 will take you up to the Culp's Hill summit via Slocum Avenue, named after Union Maj. Gen. Henry Slocum.

July 3, 1863—Pickett's Charge

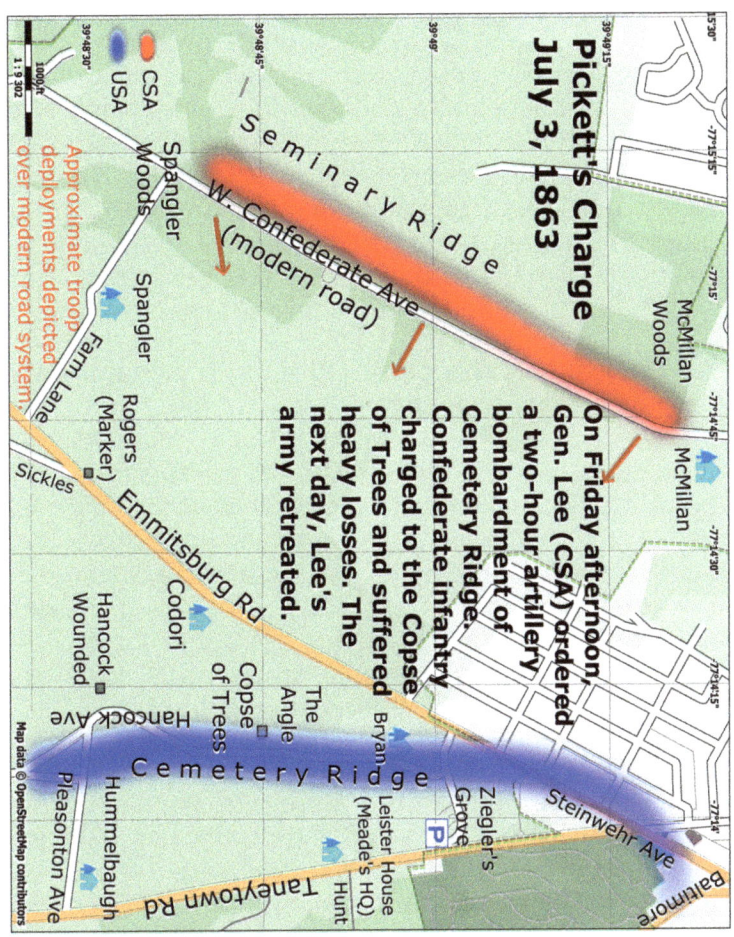

Map 1.5. July 3—Pickett's Charge

A walk in the fields of Pickett's Charge (the one-mile hike from Seminary to Cemetery Ridge) will broaden your understanding of the impact of geography on the results of the battle.

Gettysburg National Military Park

After the U.S. Civil War, former Union Maj. Gen. Daniel E. Sickles sponsored legislation to establish a national military park in Gettysburg, Pennsylvania. He introduced H.R. 8096 in 1894, and Congress approved the bill in 1895. Since that time, Gettysburg National Military Park has grown to more than 6,000 acres under the management of the National Park Service. For modern maps of park roads and geography, see Map P.2 on p. 12 and Map 1.6 on p. 21, respectively.

Today, most roads in Gettysburg National Military Park are named after Union officers of the Army of the Potomac. The shape of each park road roughly matches the battlefield formation for the soldiers under that officer's command. This park feature can be very helpful to bicyclists who want to understand the battlefield story relative to one's current location. For example, the broken and angled shape of Sickles Avenue depicts Sickles' tenuous 3rd Corps line on July 2, 1863. You can see this by matching Sickles' line shown on Map 1.3 with Sickles Avenue on Map P.2.

At Gettysburg, the NPS maintains more than 1,300 monuments and markers. There are eighteen state monuments on Seminary and Cemetery Ridges. Throughout the park stand eight large equestrian monuments (six Union and two Confederate generals) and many more bronze portrait statues. Most of Gettysburg's monuments are dedicated to regiments in the Army of the Potomac, although you will find many Confederate markers and cast-iron tablets.

Clearly, it is well beyond the scope of this mini-book to identify more than a small sampling of monuments that you will find while riding Route 2.

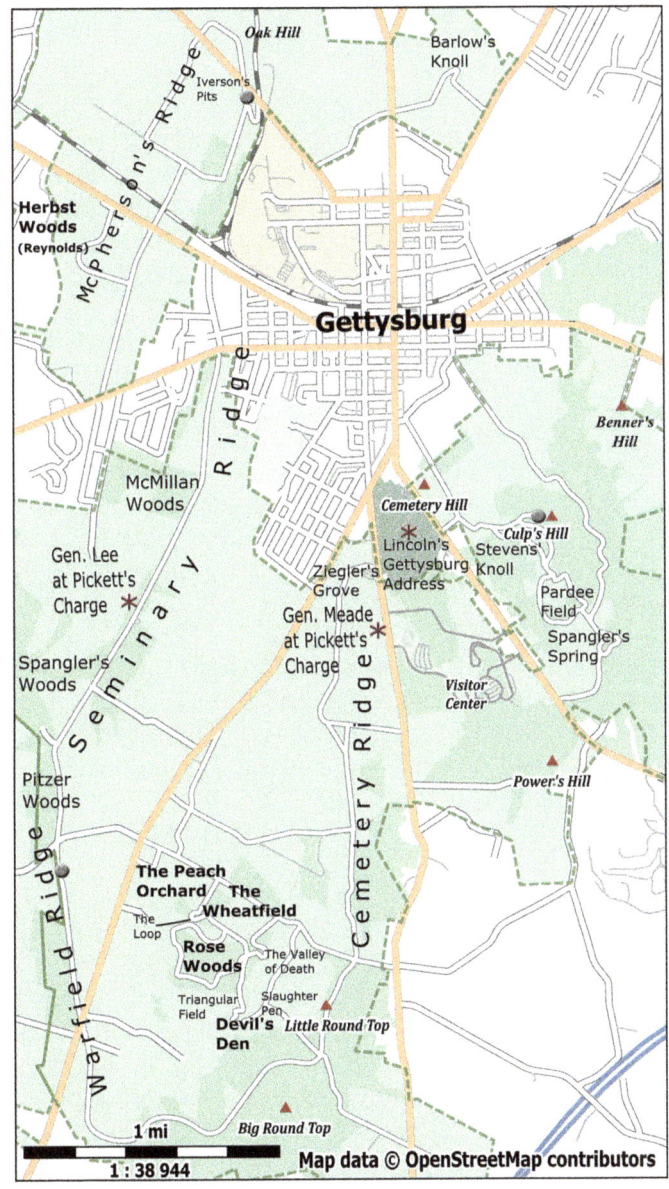

Map 1.6. Gettysburg Geography

Gettysburg National Military Park

Battle Day 1 Loop (No. 2)

Route 2, the "Battle Day 1 Loop," is a 10.5-mile ride through the fields and ridges on which two armies fought on July 1, 1863. After a tour of the northern half of the Gettysburg battlefield—one which requires some careful road-riding—you will enjoy a hilly, tree-lined tour of the slopes of Culp's Hill. See Map 1.7, p. 24.

Most Civil War Cycling routes begin and end at 945 Baltimore Pike, currently near a hotel and 0.5 miles north of the Gettysburg National Military Park (GNMP) Visitor Center. This location simplifies the design of safe, convenient, and circular routes that are composed of reusable segments (more on that, below). It is also close to the GNMP Bus/RV parking, where there are restrooms and water, and to Spangler's Spring parking.

Route 2 begins with a ride through East Cemetery Hill and a zigzag through residential roads to get to northwest Gettysburg. Here we tour McPherson's Ridge, Oak Hill, and Barlow's Knoll. Next we ride south through town to Culp's Hill, and then back to our starting point. See Map 1.6 on p. 21 and Map 1.7 on p. 24.

Understanding Segment Maps

Route 2 is one of fourteen Gettysburg bicycling routes published by Civil War Cycling. Each route is designed by chaining together a series of "segments" that function as "building blocks" for creating routes. Although Route 1 consists of Segments A through L, in order, other routes contain a different number and ordering of segments. Route 2 consists of five segments (A–E) that total 10.5 miles:

Segment A	1.6 miles
Segment B	3.5 miles
Segment C	0.6 miles
Segment D	2.3 miles
Segment E	2.5 miles
Total:	10.5 miles

The odometer readings in this book are accurate to +/- 0.05 mile but can vary based on your riding style and equipment. Also, detailed directions in the form of cue tables will help confirm your location on the battlefield.

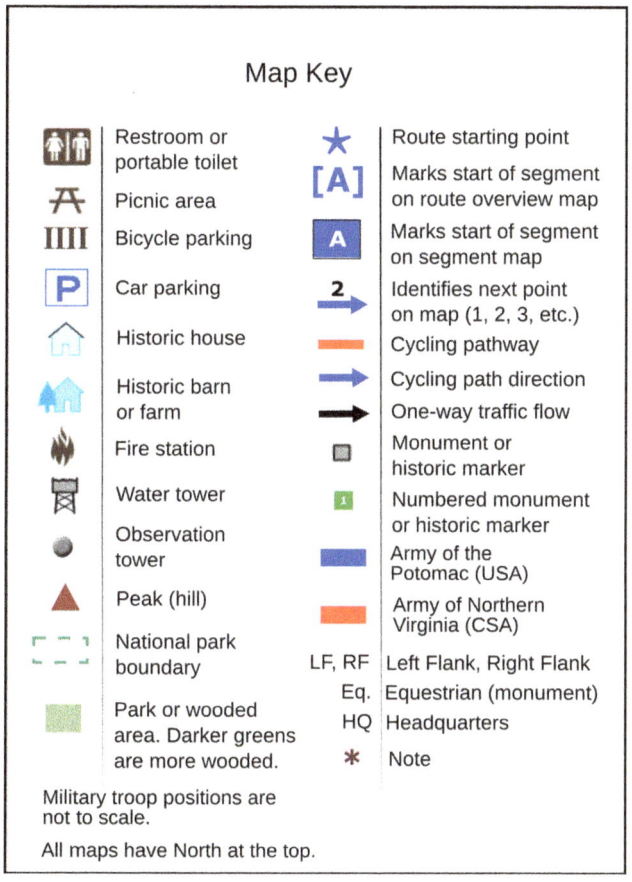

Table 1.2. Map and Symbol Key

Maps to Bike Gettysburg No. 2

Gettysburg National Military Park

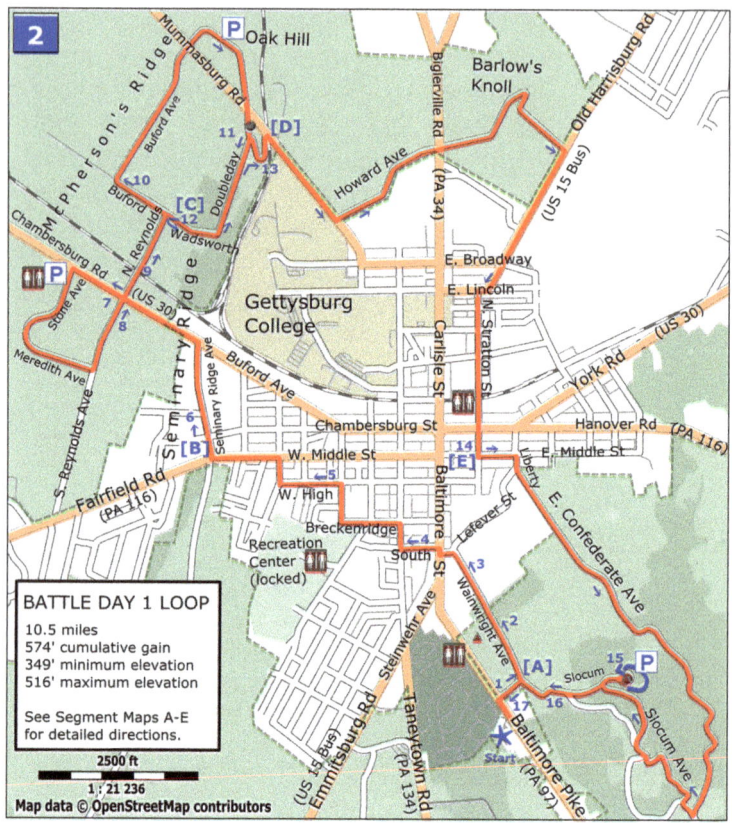

Map 1.7. Route 2 Overview Map

Maps, turn-by-turn directions, and monument highlights for each segment follow.

Tip: As will be discussed later in this chapter, National Park Service policy at Gettysburg allows bicyclists to ride against the flow of traffic. You will do that for 400-feet when you turn right on Slocum Avenue at the start of Segment A. Although cars infrequently visit this area, if you feel uncomfortable, please walk your bicycle to Wainwright Avenue.

Understanding Bicycle Cues

Bicycle "cues" are short instructions for completing a route. Each segment map has a corresponding cue table that may use these abbreviations:

◄L	Turn Left	R►	Turn Right
◄QL	Quick Left	QR►	Quick Right
◄BL	Bear Left	BR►	Bear Right
PoL	Pass on Left	PoR	Pass on Right
CS	Continue Straight	ST	Straight Through
SS	Stop Sign	TL	Traffic Light
X	Cross	U	U-Turn
DE	Dead-End	T	T Intersection
UM	Un-Marked	Y	Y Intersection
RR	Railroad	b/c	Becomes
N	North	E	East
S	South	W	West

Table 1.3. Bicycle Cue Abbreviations

Park road signs are often not located or visible at a point at which bicyclists need to make a turning decision. They are black cast iron signs that lie close to the ground. Refer to the maps and cue tables for help. Also, route detours (if any) are highlighted in gray and optionally replace the previous listed instruction.

Finding Battlefield Monuments

Segment maps have white-on-green numbers that identify a small number of featured monuments. For detailed coverage and photos of 100+ monuments, see the guidebook, *Bicycling Gettysburg National Military Park*. You can use both books together but for different purposes. For example, you could read the guidebook before your trip and carry this mini-book on your ride.

Gettysburg National Military Park

Park Bicycling Policies & Town Ordinances

The road network at Gettysburg National Military Park is designed to keep motor vehicles moving in one direction, which means there are many one-way roads. This can be a problem for bicyclists, since not having a pre-planned route can result in feeling frustrated at having to ride many miles to get to a point only a few hundred yards away. Fortunately, if you use Civil War Cycling's maps and directions, you can ride a loop that follows one-way signs. It is worth noting, however, that GNMP policies explicitly allow bicyclists to ride against the flow of traffic within the park (see Section 36, CFR 4.30, *Superintendent's Compendium*, 2016). But not everyone wants to risk confusing motor vehicle drivers.

As for sidewalks in downtown Gettysburg, bicyclists may ride on sidewalks, unless posted otherwise, but they must yield to pedestrians (Code 3-106). Please note that although Gettysburg is a relatively small town, motor vehicle traffic is often congested and bicycle lanes are rare. Even if you are an expert road cyclist, for example, the approach to the Lutheran Seminary while riding on West Middle Street can be dangerous due fast-moving truck traffic on this steep hill with no bicycle lane (but there is a sidewalk). The maps in this book will identify sidewalk options for your consideration.

At the Gettysburg Museum & Visitor Center, "riders should walk their bikes while on pedestrian walks and trails." Not surprisingly, off-road riding is prohibited (www.nps.gov/gett/planyourvisit) in GNMP. You may walk your bicycle at the national cemetery. And finally, check the "Alerts & Conditions" page on the park website before your ride; this site is regularly updated: https://www.nps.gov/gett/planyourvisit/conditions.htm.

2. Let's Go! Bike Route 2

Route 2 Synopsis

Difficulty	Moderate (requires road-cycling)
Time	3–4 hours (frequent stops)
Distance	10.5 miles
Cumulative Gain	574 feet
Historical Focus	July 1, 1863
Geography	McPherson's Ridge, Oak Hill, Barlow's Knoll, Culp's Hill
Safety	Mix of public and park roads (2.9 miles on busy town streets)

Similarities Between Routes 1–3

Civil War Cycling's routes provide a historical context and focus for your battlefield ride. You can select routes based on how and what you want to learn or experience. And you can also assemble a set of routes to design a multi-day tour.

Route 2, the "Battle Day 1 Loop," is ideal for bicyclists who want to break Route 1's full day tour into two separate rides—Route 2 (10.5 miles) on one day and Route 5 (12.2 miles) on the next. Or for an expanded tour that includes complete coverage of Culp's Hill, you might want to consider pairing Route 2 and Route 3 (17.0 miles). As a bonus, Routes 1 and 3 also include abbreviated options (1b, 11.5 miles and 3b, 10.7 miles) that skip Warfield Ridge and South Cavalry Field. For more planning help, please visit www.civilwarcycling.com/battlefields/gettysburg/routes/.

Gettysburg National Military Park

Segment A (East Cemetery Hill)

Map 2.1. Route 2 Segment A (1.6 miles)

Remember: White-on-green numbers identify monuments whose photos are on the following pages.

28 Battle Day 1 Loop

Segment A Cues (1.6 miles)

From 945 Baltimore Pike to north end of W. Confederate Avenue:		Seg	Total
0.0	RIGHT on Slocum (400 feet against traffic)	0.1	**0.1**
0.1	LEFT on Wainwright to tour East Cemetery Hill, to stop sign at Lefever	0.5	**0.5**
0.5	LEFT at Lefever to Baltimore. CROSS to sidewalk	0.5	**0.5**
	RIGHT onto sidewalk, then quick LEFT on South for 1 block	0.7	**0.7**
0.7	RIGHT on S. Washington for 1 block to Breckenridge	0.8	**0.8**
0.8	LEFT on Breckenridge to dead-end at West	1.0	**1.0**
1.0	RIGHT on West for 1 block to stop sign at W. High	1.1	**1.1**
1.1	LEFT on W. High to dead-end on Howard	1.3	**1.3**
1.3	RIGHT on Howard for 1 block	1.4	**1.4**
1.4	CROSS W. Middle to *sidewalk* and then LEFT up steep hill to traffic light. This can be a dangerous stretch of road for cyclists.	1.6	**1.6**

Table 2.1. Segment A Cues

Segment A Monument Highlights

For each route segment, this book provides photos and short descriptions for a sampling of monuments. Numbers on the map match-up to photo numbers. GPS coordinates (lat, lon) are listed above each photo.

Gettysburg National Military Park

1. 39.81990, -77.22617

2. 39.82098, -77.22875

3. 39.82132, -77.22889

4. 39.82165, -77.22888

5. 39.82195, -77.22888

6. 39.82264, -77.22811

1. 33rd Massachusetts Monument (1885)

With the 5th Maine Artillery Battery, the 33rd Massachusetts decimated the 57th North Carolina regiment as the Tar Heels attacked from the east, and as the Louisiana Tigers fired cannons from the north.

2. 4th Ohio Monument (1887)

According to the monument inscription, the 4th Ohio was "hotly engaged in support of batteries on East Cemetery Hill until after 10 P.M." on July 2, 1863.

3. Winfield Hancock Equestrian Monument (1895–6)

Winfield Scott Hancock, nicknamed "Hancock the Superb," was a Pennsylvania native. He commanded the 2nd Corps of the Army of the Potomac, and was wounded southwest of here, during Pickett's Charge.

4. Oliver O. Howard Headquarters Monument

Maj. Gen. Howard established his headquarters on the high ground of East Cemetery Hill after ceding the town to the Army of Northern Virginia on July 1.

5. Oliver O. Howard Equestrian Monument (1932)

Oliver Otis Howard was from Maine. He commanded the 11th Corps of the Army of the Potomac, a group of mostly German immigrants.

6. 17th Connecticut Monument (1889)

On July 1, after retreating south from Barlow's Knoll, the 17th Connecticut fought here on East Cemetery Hill. Their commander, Lt. Col. Douglas Fowler, died from artillery fire while riding his white horse on the knoll.

Gettysburg National Military Park

Landscape Views

While standing at the first monument, look southeast to Culp's Hill, shown below. Then turn to your left to view the field over which the 57th North Carolina attacked Col. Adin B. Underwood's men from Massachusetts, who were supported by Capt. Greenleaf T. Stevens' artillery battery from Maine. The knoll on which you stand is named for Capt. Stevens.

On your ride north on Wainwright Avenue, you will pass East Cemetery Hill on your left. Although you can quickly identify monuments on the hill, you may want to stop to explore on foot. (There are no bicycle racks).

Notably, the Hancock Equestrian Monument (3) stands on the hill's peak, and the nearby water tower is a helpful orienteering landmark. The tower is visible from several positions on the battlefield. For example, if you visit Benner's Hill (Latimer Avenue) by car, you will see that Confederate guns point to East Cemetery Hill.

Gettysburg National Military Park

Segment B (The Ridge to Oak Hill)

Segment B 3.5 miles

Ride north to tour McPherson's Ridge. Here on July 1, 1863, Confederate infantry fought Union cavalry until the Union 1st Corps arrived.

Map 2.2. Route 2 Segment B (3.5 miles)

Battle Day 1 Loop

Segment B Cues (3.5 miles)

	North on Seminary Ridge Avenue to Tour McPherson's Ridge:	Seg	Total
0.0	From light at W. Middle, RIGHT on Seminary Ridge to dead-end	0.3	**1.9**
0.3	LEFT on Buford (US 30) for 0.3 miles to traffic light	0.6	**2.2**
0.6	STRAIGHT at light (now Chambersburg Road) for 0.2 miles	0.8	**2.4**
0.8	*Careful* LEFT on Stone-Meredith at seasonal Visitor Center for 0.5 miles	1.3	**2.9**
1.3	LEFT on S. Reynolds at dead-end (stop) for 0.25 miles to traffic light	1.55	**3.15**
1.55	STRAIGHT to cross Chambersburg, then 0.25 miles to stop at Buford	1.8	**3.4**
1.8	LEFT on Buford Avenue for 0.7 miles to Mummasburg Road stop sign	2.5	**4.1**
2.5	STRAIGHT on N. Confederate for 0.4 miles to Mummasburg Road again	2.9	**4.5**
2.9	STRAIGHT on Doubleday for 0.4 miles, then 0.2 miles on Wadsworth	3.5	**5.1**
3.5	TURN AROUND for Segment C (or loop around to Oak Tower again!)	3.5	**5.1**

Table 2.2. Segment B Cues

Please ride safely on Chambersburg Pike (US 30).

Gettysburg National Military Park

Although the shoulders are wide, cars are fast-moving.

Segment B Monument Highlights

1. 39.83211, -77.24457

2. 39.83490, -77.24546

3. 39.83790, -77.25136

4. 39.83789, -77.25167

5. 39.83592, -77.25269

6. 39.83493, -77.25440

1. Lutheran Theological Seminary

Early on July 1, 1863, Union cavalry officer Brig. Gen. John Buford looked west to survey the Confederate army from the top of the seminary cupola.

2. Robert E. Lee Headquarters Monument

Gen. Lee, Commander of the Army of Northern Virginia, established his headquarters in this area. He stayed at the nearby home of a seventy-year-old widow, Mrs. Mary Thompson.

3. John F. Reynolds Equestrian Monument (1899)

Gen. Meade, Commander of the Army of the Potomac, put Pennsylvania native Maj. Gen. Reynolds in charge of the army's left wing (1st, 3rd, 11th Corps).

4. John Buford Statue (1895)

On July 1, Buford's cavalry division held the Confederate army at bay until Union 1st Corps infantry arrived on McPherson's Ridge. His principal opponent was Maj. Gen. Henry Heth's infantry division.

5. John L. Burns Statue (1903)

A sixty-nine-year-old Gettysburg citizen, Burns joined the battle on July 1 when he attached himself to the 150th Pennsylvania and later the Iron Brigade.

6. 24th Michigan (1889)

Organized in Detroit, the 24th Michigan was part of the Iron Brigade—iron-willed fighters from Michigan, Indiana, and Wisconsin, who on July 1 challenged attackers from North Carolina, Alabama, and Tennessee in Herbst (now Reynolds') Woods.

Gettysburg National Military Park

7. 39.83472, -77.25461

8. 39.83417, -77.25094

9. 39.83579, -77.24947

10. 39.84850, -77.24336

11. 39.84439, -77.24200

12. 39.84400, -77.24194

13. 39.84222, -77.24256

The Eternal Light Peace Memorial (10) stands on high-ground from which you can see McPherson's Ridge (to your right) as well as Union positions along modern-day Doubleday Avenue (to your left). From the observation tower (12), Barlow's Knoll is faintly visible to the east.

7. 26th North Carolina Monument (1985)

At Gettysburg, the 26th North Carolina suffered 687 casualties out of 839 men.

8. John F. Reynolds Killed Monument (1886)

On the morning of July 1, while rallying infantry to relieve Buford's cavalry, Maj. Gen. Reynolds was shot in the neck, dying instantly near this spot. He was the highest ranking officer killed at the Battle of Gettysburg.

9. 8th Illinois Cavalry Monument (1891)

This monument marks the July 1 battlefield position of 470 cavalrymen from Illinois.

10. Eternal Light Peace Memorial (1938)

President Franklin D. Roosevelt dedicated this memorial on the battle's 75th anniversary.

11. 90th Pennsylvania Monument (1888)

This monument honors the legendary actions of a 90th Pennsylvania soldier who—on seeing a bird's nest thrown from a tree—returned it while under heavy fire.

12. Oak Ridge Observation Tower (1895)

Designed by E. B. Cope, this tower was cut to twenty-three feet and its roof removed in the 1960s.

13. 11th Pennsylvania Monument (1889)

The 11th Pennsylvania Monument faces the field through which Iverson's North Carolinians attacked. It includes a bronze sculpture of the regiment's dog, Sallie, who survived the battle but not the war.

Gettysburg National Military Park

Landscape Views

The Reynolds Equestrian Monument (3) in both photos, below, faces the South Mountain gap through which Confederate Maj. Gen. Heth's infantry attacked Union Brig. Gen. Buford's cavalry on July 1, 1863.

The McPherson barn stands on the ridge.

Battle Day 1 Loop

Aside from the prominence of Oak Hill at the north end of Seminary Ridge, the most helpful orienteering landmarks in northwest Gettysburg are tall physical structures like the Eternal Light Peace Memorial and the Oak Ridge Observation Tower. From both places, you can see much of the July 1 battlefield. (Below, the cannon near the memorial points toward the tower).

Confederate Cannon on Oak Hill Pointing to Doubleday Avenue

Union 1st Corps Battle Line (Doubleday Avenue) on July 1, 1863

View from the Oak Hill Observation Tower Looking Northwest to the Eternal Light Peace Memorial

Gettysburg National Military Park

Segment C (Return to Tower)

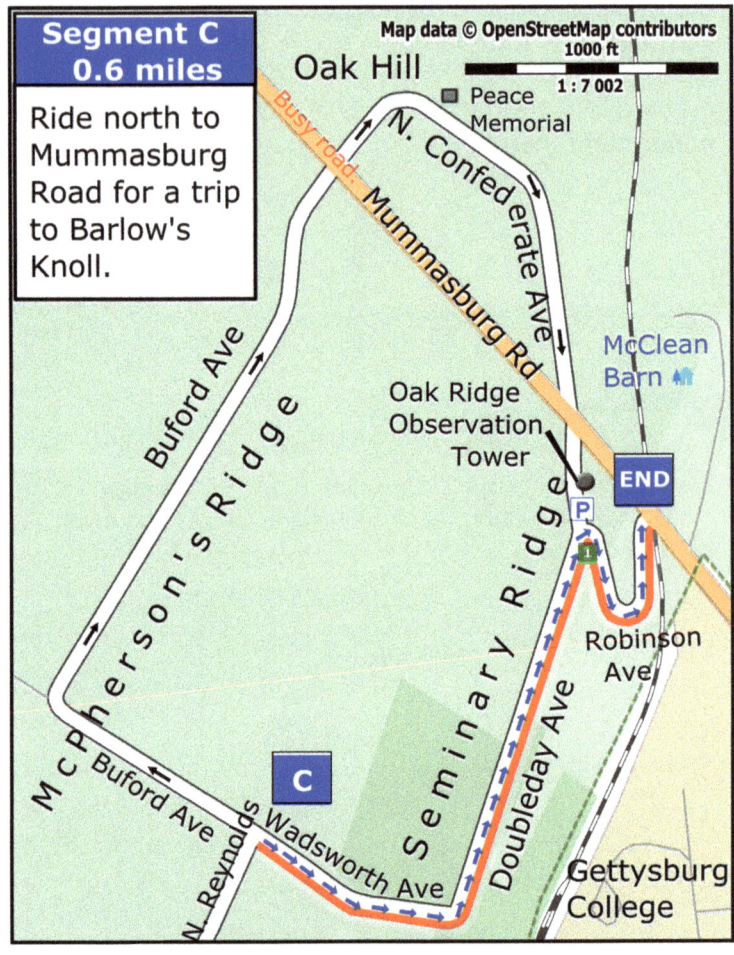

Map 2.3. Route 2 Segment C (0.6 miles)

Segment C is a 0.6-mile ride that doubles back to the observation tower to connect to Mummasburg Road via Robinson Avenue. This is the easiest way to tour all of Doubleday Avenue, without skipping Barlow's Knoll, which is about 1.1 miles to the east.

Segment C Cues (0.6 miles)

Return to Mummasburg Road (for tour of Barlow's Knoll):		Seg	Total
0.0	From Wadsworth at Buford, face east and ride 0.4 miles	0.4	**5.5**
0.4	Sharp RIGHT on Robinson, *carefully* down blind curve 0.2 miles to stop	0.6	**5.7**

Table 2.3. Segment C Cues

Robinson Avenue is a two-way blind curve that impairs your visibility to motor vehicles; be careful riding down to Mummasburg Road. Also, the gravel on the side of Mummasburg Road can be thick and unsteady for bicyclists. The road is reasonably safe.

Segment C Monument Highlights

1. 39.84347, -77.24187 — **John C. Robinson Statue (1917)**

From Binghamton, New York, John Cleveland Robinson (1817–97) led the 2nd Division, 1st Corps against the Confederate assault on Oak Ridge on July 1. The Robinson statue stands on modern-day Robinson Avenue, where his division fought on July 1, 1863.

Gettysburg National Military Park

Landscape Views

From Oak Ridge Observation Tower, look south toward the Robinson statue. (See the photo, below). From this viewpoint, the field to the right of Doubleday Avenue is "Iverson's Pits," named for Brig. Gen. Alfred Iverson's North Carolina brigade, Rodes' division. On July 1, 1863, many Confederate soldiers died in this field during their assault from Oak Hill. The monuments along this road honor Union regiments from Massachusetts, Maine, New York, and Pennsylvania.

Robinson Avenue is on the left side of the above photo. In the distant left you can see Gettysburg College and the Lutheran Seminary, which like most Gettysburg area properties became field hospitals during and immediately after the battle.

Next, look left again for an eastward view from the observation tower. Then scan the horizon to spot a tall, thin radio tower. (It stands near Old Harrisburg Road). Slightly to the left of that structure is Barlow's Knoll. On July 1, the Union battle line extended from where you are currently standing to a little more than one mile east to the knoll. Originally named Blocher's Knoll, this slightly elevated patch of land was renamed after the Civil War to honor Brig. Gen. Francis C. Barlow, whose job it was to hold the Union right flank on July 1.

Finally, look left again and note the red barn on the east side of the railroad tracks. This is McClean farm. Two brothers named Schwarz—each of whom had emigrated from Germany but moved to different parts of the country (New York and Alabama)—met somewhere near the McClean property in July, 1863. Rudolph Schwarz fought for the Union and died from his wounds; his Confederate brother was captured.

Gettysburg National Military Park

Segment D (Barlow's Knoll)

Map 2.4. Route 2 Segment D (2.3 miles)

**Segment D
2.3 miles**

In the late afternoon on July 1, Gen. Howard's Union line collapsed. We travel that line to Barlow's Knoll, and then ride south along a path of retreat.

North of downtown Gettysburg, Howard Avenue traces Union Maj. Gen. Howard's 11th Corps battle line—specifically that of his 1st Division commander, Brig. Gen. Francis C. Barlow.

Battle Day 1 Loop

Segment D Cues (2.3 miles)

**Mummasburg Road
to Barlow's Knoll, Then South Through Town:**   Seg   Total

0.0	From Robinson dead-end, RIGHT on Mummasburg for 0.3 miles	0.3	**6.0**
0.3	LEFT on Howard for 0.4 miles to stop at Biglerville Road (PA 34)	0.7	**6.4**
0.7	CROSS Biglerville Road. One-way for 0.4 miles to Barlow's Knoll	1.1	**6.8**
1.1	Round bend on Howard for 0.2 miles to dead-end at Old Harrisburg	1.3	**7.0**
1.3	RIGHT onto sidewalk on Old Harrisburg Road (Business 15) for 0.4 miles	1.7	**7.4**
1.7	Pass E. Broadway on right and bend RIGHT on E. Lincoln for a few feet	1.8	**7.5**
1.8	FIRST LEFT on N. Stratton and then ride 0.3 miles to railroad tracks. Detour: At the 1.9-mile-point is Coster Avenue; turn left to visit the 154th New York Monument.	2.1	**7.8**
2.1	CROSS railroad tracks and then ride 0.1 miles to York	2.2	**7.9**
2.2	CROSS York and then ride 0.1 miles to E. Middle	2.3	**8.0**

Table 2.4. Segment D Cues

Note: There is a public restroom at the Gettysburg Transit Station on Carlisle Street.

Gettysburg National Military Park

Tourist traffic on Howard Avenue is very light. The roads are smooth and flat for bicycling, but have hardly any shade trees. When Howard Avenue dead-ends at Old Harrisburg Road, you will see a supermarket and community college in the plaza across the road. At this point, you may want to consider riding on the sidewalk for about 1.3 miles, which is the balance of this bicycling segment. Finally, if you take the Coster Avenue detour, this grassy area is often wet with dew that can soak your shoes.

Segment D Monument Highlights

1. 39.84549, -77.22648

2. 39.83511, -77.22750

3. 39.83200, -77.22870

The Amos Humiston Memorial (3) is in the same lot as the Gettysburg Fire Department, on the south side of the railroad tracks. Humiston is buried in New York Plot B-14 of the national military cemetery at Gettysburg (39.82069, -77.23139).

1. Francis C. Barlow Statue (1922)

Barlow graduated first in his class at Harvard University and practiced law for the New York Tribune newspaper. Wounded in his left side at the Battle of Gettysburg, Brig. Gen. Barlow was a twenty-eight-year-old officer in Howard's 11th Corps. His division was the right flank of the Union army when his line collapsed.

2. 154th New York Monument (1890)

The 154th New York was attached to Col. Charles R. Coster's 1st Brigade, which provided covering fire for the Union army as it retreated through town the afternoon of July 1, 1863. The monument is in a grassy area at the end of Coster Avenue, behind a mural by artists Mark H. Dunkelman and Johan Bjurman. Dedicated in 1988 (and restored in 2002 and 2015), the mural depicts the hand-to-hand combat that erupted between Coster's men and Confederate troops under Hays and Avery. Over 700 men were killed here.

Gettysburg National Military Park

3. Amos Humiston Memorial (1993)

The 154th New York suffered 83 percent casualties, of which Sgt. Amos Humiston was one. He died while clutching an image of his three young children. Erected by Gettysburg citizens, it is the only battlefield memorial for an enlisted man.

Segment D Landscape View

At Barlow's Knoll, you will find several cannons that point toward the attack led by Confederate Maj. Gen. Jubal E. Early, Ewell's Corps. Their barrels are green due to bronze oxidation. Called "Napoleons" for their use in the Napoleonic Wars in Europe, these are smoothbore (non-rifled) guns. The monument on the right side of the next photo was erected by the 17th Connecticut regiment, led by Lt. Col. Douglas Fowler, who died on the knoll after being hit by an artillery shell. (Note: The radio tower in the distance is visible from the observation tower on Oak Ridge).

July 1, 1863, ended with the collapse of the Union line and retreat to high ground at East Cemetery Hill and nearby Culp's Hill, our next biking segment.

Bonus Map—Downtown Gettysburg

Map 2.5. Downtown Gettysburg

Although as of this writing downtown Gettysburg is somewhat challenging to bike, the ride is certainly manageable for safety-conscious adults. The town is gradually repairing its residential roads and sidewalks. In some areas bike chevrons are being painted onto roads to encourage bicyclists to "take the lane." Even so, you may find that Gettysburg is best for walking tourists, whereas its national park is ideal for bicyclists.

Gettysburg National Military Park

Segment E (Culp's Hill Area)

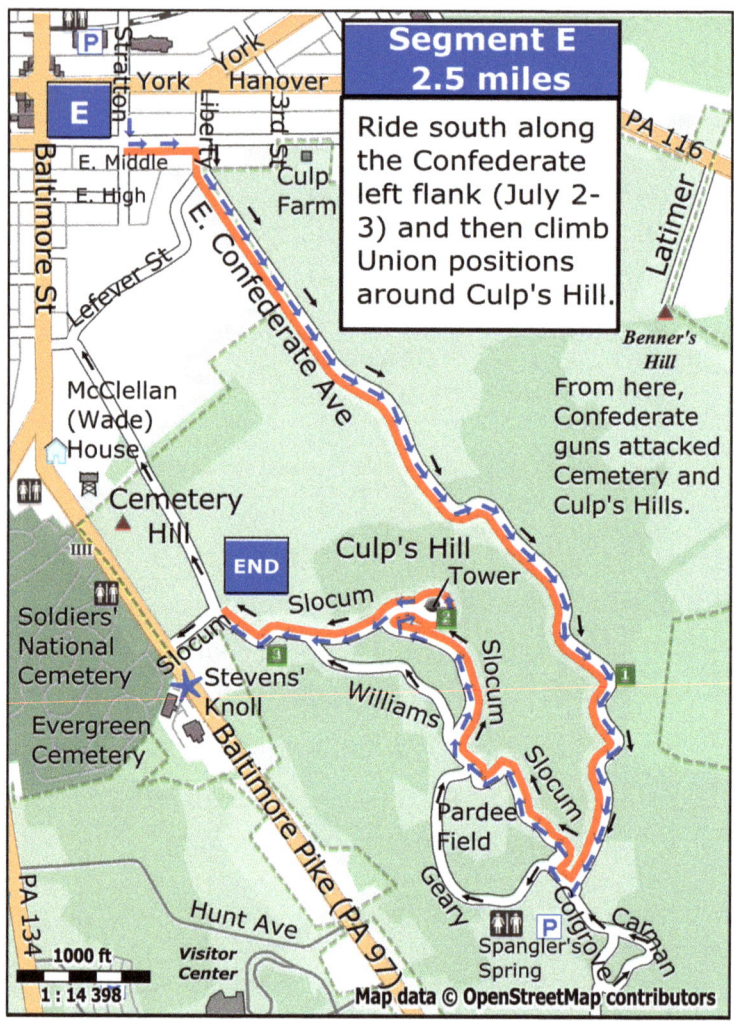

Map 2.6. Route 2 Segment E (2.5 miles)

The ride down E. Confederate Avenue follows the scenic contour of the Confederate battle line.

Battle Day 1 Loop

Segment E Cues (2.5 miles)

	E. Middle Street **to Culp's Hill Via E. Confederate Avenue:**	Seg	Total
0.0	From E. Middle at N. Stratton, LEFT on E. Middle for 0.1 miles	0.1	**8.1**
0.1	STRAIGHT on E. Confederate for 1.4 miles to dead-end at Colgrove	1.5	**9.5**
1.5	RIGHT into Spangler's Spring. RIGHT at fork on Slocum for 0.3 miles	1.8	**9.8**
1.8	Pass Geary on left, then bear RIGHT uphill on Slocum for 0.4 miles	2.2	**10.2**
2.2	At dead-end, RIGHT uphill to Culp's Hill tower, around and down	2.3	**10.3**
2.3	Down, passing Slocum and Williams to Wainwright after 0.2 miles	2.5	**10.5**

Table 2.5. Segment E Cues

After a 0.1-mile ride on E. Middle Street, Segment E meets a confusing intersection. Look for the brown National Park Service sign that marks the beginning of E. Confederate Avenue. Car traffic is light on this shady, up and down ride along the east slope of Culp's Hill, which is not part of the official park auto tour.

Spangler's Spring is a good place to stop to rest before starting the climb up Culp's Hill. You can sit on the stone walls in the parking lot. (Pack extra trash bags to carry your garbage out of the park). The nearby stone building is a good restroom. Please note

Gettysburg National Military Park

that park restrooms and portable toilets are open on a seasonal basis; see www.nps.gov//gett/planyourvisit.

The ride up Slocum Avenue to the summit can be disorienting, so when in doubt, veer to the right. If you walk your bike up this steep hill, you can visit many regimental monuments. On the ride back down, watch for cars merging from your left before bottoming out at Stevens' Knoll near the Slocum Equestrian monument.

Segment E Monument Highlights

1. 39.81852, -77.21551

North Carolinians attacked Culp's Hill from this spot.

2. 39.81983, -77.22008

3. 39.81908, -77.22458

At Gettysburg, eight equestrian monuments honor Union (6) and Confederate (2) corps commanders. The one at the base of Culp's Hill in Stevens' Knoll honors right wing (12th Corps) commander Henry "Slow Come" Slocum, USA.

1. 43rd North Carolina Monument (1988)

The 43rd North Carolina Monument marks the location of the regiment's uphill attack at the base of Culp's Hill. A storm of bullets from Candy and Kane's brigades of Geary's division stopped them.

2. George S. Greene Statue (1907)

At sixty-two years old, Brig. Gen. George "Pop" Greene was the oldest Union general at Gettysburg. On July 2, Greene's New Yorkers built breastworks and held the Union right against a Confederate division.

3. Henry W. Slocum Equestrian Monument (1907)

Located in a knoll between Cemetery and Culp's Hills, this monument honors Maj. Gen. Slocum, the 12th Corps commander who held the Union right flank at Culp's Hill. Here, you can see the monument at the high point of the knoll on Slocum Avenue.

Gettysburg National Military Park

Landscape Views

From Spangler's Spring, the following photo shows the start of the climb up Slocum Avenue, where you will reach the Culp's Hill summit and tower in 0.75 miles.

The second photo shows a distant view of the west side of Culp's Hill, as seen from East Cemetery Hill near Baltimore Pike. In both locations, Union infantry and artillery fought defensively against Lt. Gen. Richard S. Ewell's late afternoon and evening attacks. By the late morning of the following day, July 3, Ewell was defeated—despite Confederate cannon fire from Benner's Hill in the early afternoon.

Views from the Culp's Hill Tower

The first photo shows the view looking northwest from the tower; the second is looking southwest.

Gettysburg National Military Park has three 19th-century steel observation towers that provide a commanding view of the battlefield. One is on Culp's Hill, and the others are on Warfield Ridge (Longstreet tower) and Oak Ridge. Although there are currently no bicycle racks at any of these towers, it is worth your effort to figure out how to secure your bikes so that you can walk up the stairs to the observation decks. Bring this book with you to help identify historic landmarks.

Gettysburg National Military Park

3. What Next?

You did it! You cycled 10.5 miles through the Gettysburg battlefield and learned about what happened here on July 1, 1863—the first of three days of fighting between the Union Army of the Potomac and the Confederate Army of Northern Virginia. You learned about the Battle of Gettysburg while riding through the wooded area of McPherson's Ridge and north along Seminary Ridge to Oak Hill; then down to Barlow's Knoll, through town, and ending with a tour of the Confederate and Union battle lines around Culp's Hill.

I sincerely hope that you want to return to Gettysburg and to explore more of its rich natural and physical landmarks, including more than 1,300 monuments and 400 refurbished Civil War cannons. In preparation for your next visit—or maybe to revive memories of your most recent ride—you will want to consult *Bicycling Gettysburg National Military Park: The Cyclist's Civil War Travel Guide*. This information-packed book describes a 23.8-mile tour of the entire park and includes numerous color photos of landmarks and historical monuments.

Guidebooks by Sue Thibodeau:

ISBN 9781732603806

286 pp, full-color
6"x9" perfect bound pbk

Published March 2019
by Civil War Cycling

www.civilwarcycling.com

Available for order at
your favorite book seller.

ISBN 9781732603813

208 pp, full-color
6"x9" perfect bound pbk

Published November
2020 by Civil War
Cycling

www.civilwarcycling.com

Available for order at
your favorite book seller.

Forthcoming Publications:

Bicycling Chickamauga Battlefield (2021)

Bicycling Shiloh National Military Park (2022)

www.ingramcontent.com/pod-product-compliance
Lightning Source LLC
Chambersburg PA
CBHW061731070526
44583CB00024B/3098